That's Cool!

Great Idea!

Lucky You!

You Did It!

Love It!

Way to Go!

Brilliant!

First Place!

Ready for School!

A+

Well Done!

Beautiful!

Brilliant!

Superstar!

Ready for School!

Fabulous!

Far Out!

Super!

Soaring High!

Great Idea!

Out of this World!

Excellent!

Ready for School!

Love It!

Brilliant!

Beautiful!

A+

Ready for School!

Beautiful!

Shine Bright!

Brilliant!

Love It!

COOL!

Great Idea!

Sweet!

Terrific!

Dear Parents and Educators,

The Learnalots™ were created for kids, but we think you will love them too! They deliver important educational content through fun and engaging activities.

The Learnalots are mascots for learning essential subjects, as defined by national early learning standards. We place special emphasis on math and literacy, since they are fundamental to academic success, and also include subjects such as science, creative arts, music, social skills, health and fitness, and nature. This workbook focuses on Colors and Shapes.

We are dedicated to ensuring that our products provide a broad and rich learning experience for young children. Building a child's confidence and enthusiasm for learning at an early age is critical to future success. It is our sincere hope that the Learnalots will inspire children, and those who care for them, to learn something new every day.

~ The Learnalot Team

Thank you for making us part of your child's early learning experience. We welcome your thoughts and feedback.

What Color is it?

Trace the name of the color that describes each picture pair.

Blue

Red

What Color is it?

Trace the name of the color that describes each picture pair.

Impressive!

Toadally Awesome!

Great Idea!

Green

Yellow

What Color is it?

Trace the name of the color that describes each picture pair.

Orange

Pink

What Color is it?

Trace the name of the color that describes each picture pair.

Purple

Brown

Red Chalk

Circle the pictures that Zak drew with red chalk.

Inky Insects

Draw a line to connect each insect with its matching color.

Monster Splash

Draw a line to connect each monster with its matching color splash.

Hooray!

Rainbow Dots

Sunshine and rain combine to create rainbows.
Connect the color dots to finish coloring the rainbow.

Color with Green

Color these pictures green.

Where is My Wing?

Draw a line to match each butterfly with its missing wing.

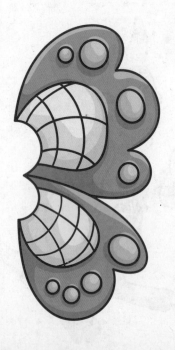  

Kimonos

Kimonos are traditional Japanese robes worn for special occasions. **Color** them.

Fruit and Veggie Colors

Which is the correct color for each fruit and vegetable?
Color the fruits and vegetables.

corn

apple

carrot

lemon

eggplant

cherry

pineapple

Awesome!

pumpkin

grapes

pepper

orange

banana

pear

broccoli

watermelon

kiwi

15

Rainbow Xylophone

Piper got a new xylophone! **Color** each bar a different color.

Getting Warm!

Zak needs help coloring his fire.
Use **warm colors** like red, orange, and yellow to **color** the flames.

Sparkle and Shine

Color the stones in the jewelry.

Bakery Treats

Color the frosting on these desserts!

Boats Afloat!

Draw a line between the sails and their matching sailboats.

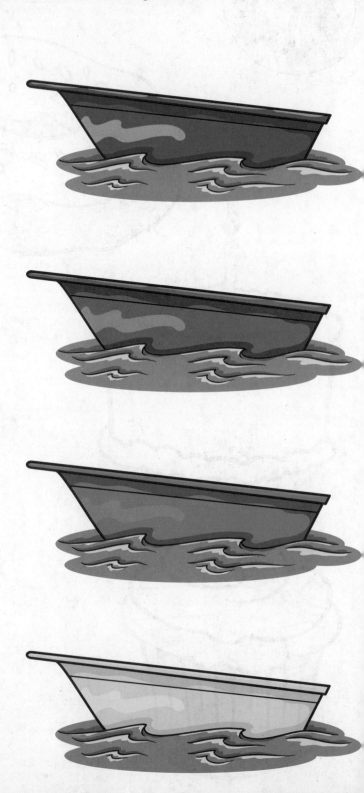

Summer Sprinkler Splash

Use the color words to help you **finish** coloring the picture.

yellow

purple

orange

green

blue

red

Find the Monsters

Find the monsters below and **color** them each a different color.

red   blue   yellow   green   orange

Houses and Hats

These hats and houses have the same patterns.
Draw a line to connect each hat to its matching house.

Flower Power

Finish these flowers with the colors of your choice.

Healthy Patterns

Fruits and vegetables have patterns inside them. **Draw a line** to match the insides to the outsides.

Apple

Kiwi

Tomato

Orange

Lemon

Watermelon

Mixing Colors

Circle the color Zak will make by mixing together red and yellow clay.

Eat a Rainbow

It is healthy to eat foods from all the colors of the rainbow.
Color each rainbow stripe to match the color of the fruit.

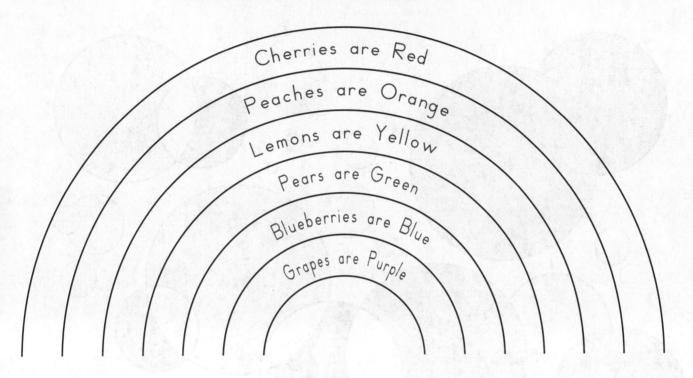

Cherries are Red

Peaches are Orange

Lemons are Yellow

Pears are Green

Blueberries are Blue

Grapes are Purple

Colored Bubbles

What colors do these bubbles make when they mix? **Color** the bubbles.

Colorful Veggie Pairs

Draw a line to connect the vegetables that have matching colors.

Nature's Colors

Nature comes in all colors of the rainbow.
How many of each color do you see on both pages? **Write** the number in each box.

Color Words: Blue

Color the word its correct color.

Blue

Color Words: Green

Color the word its correct color.

Color Words: Pink

Color the word its correct color.

Color Words: Yellow

Color the word its correct color.

Yellow

Super Shapes

Learn new shapes with Kit. **Trace** each shape.
Then, **color** each shape to look like the matching object.

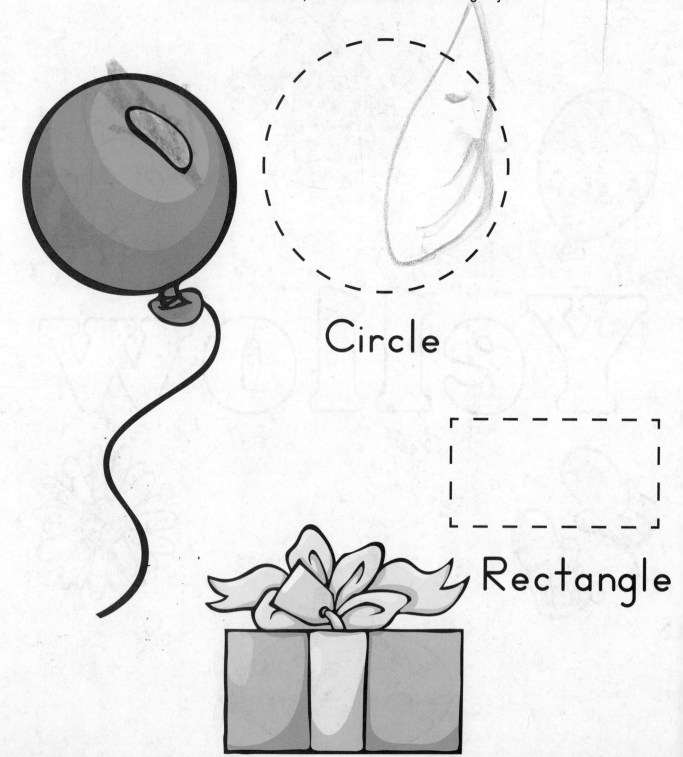

Circle

Rectangle

Square

Triangle

Rocket Shapes

Help Leo paint the rocket.
Color the shapes on the rocket to match the ones below.

circle

rectangle

triangle

square

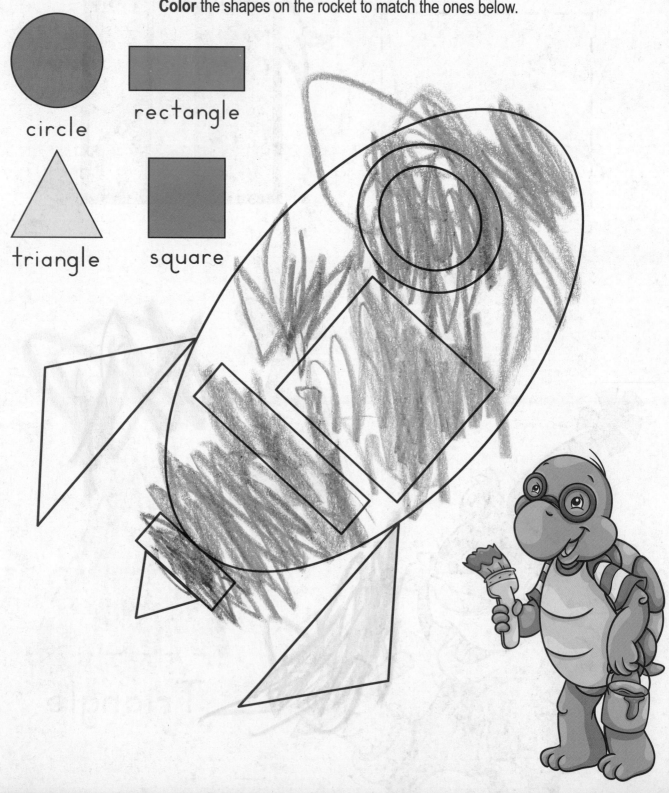

How Many Sides?

Trace each shape. **Count** the number of sides each shape has and **write** the number inside.
Circle the shape that has the most sides.

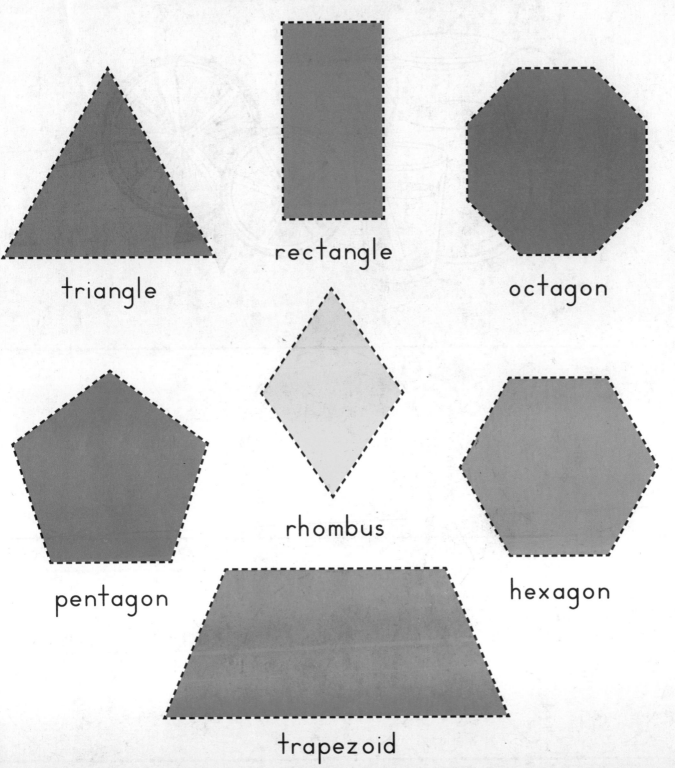

triangle

rectangle

octagon

rhombus

pentagon

hexagon

trapezoid

Tracing Shapes: Circles

Trace the circle shapes. **Color** them to make lemon and lime slices.

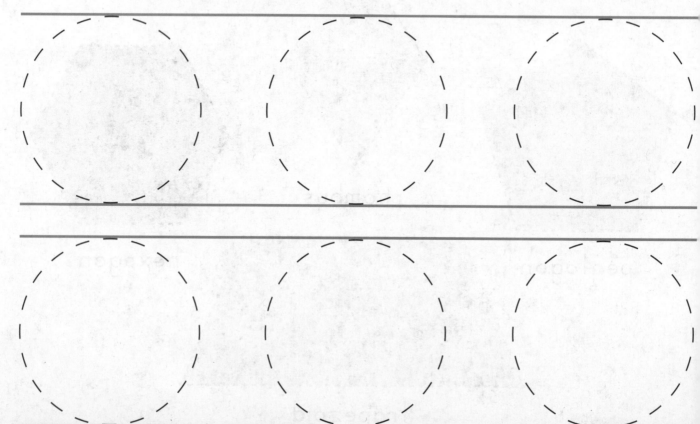

Tracing Shapes: Squares

Trace the square shapes. **Color** them to make more waffles.

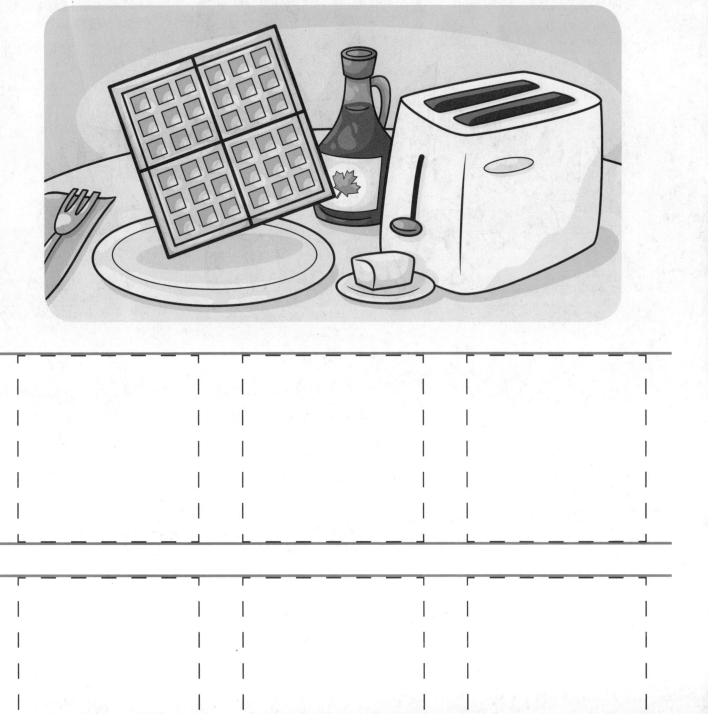

Tracing Shapes: Triangles

Trace the triangle shapes. **Color** them to make more dinosaur spikes.

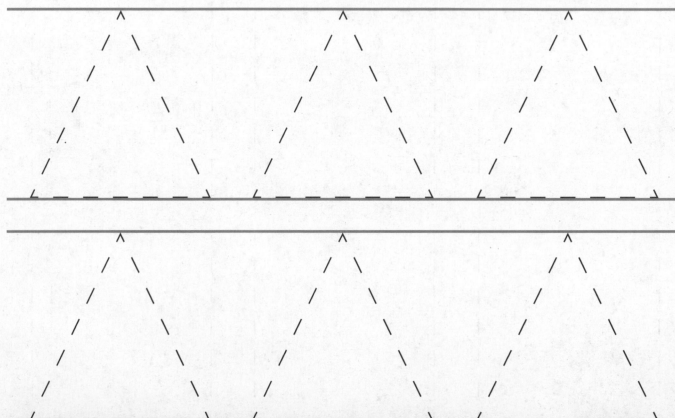

Tracing Shapes: Ovals

Trace the oval shapes. **Color** them to make more watermelons.

Tracing Shapes: Stars

Trace the star shapes. **Color** them to make more stars.

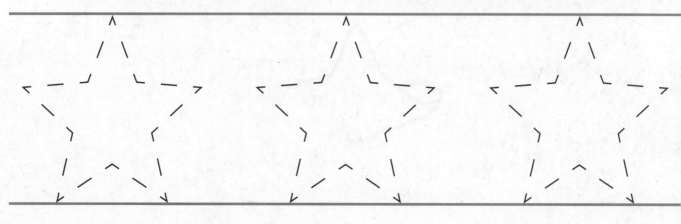

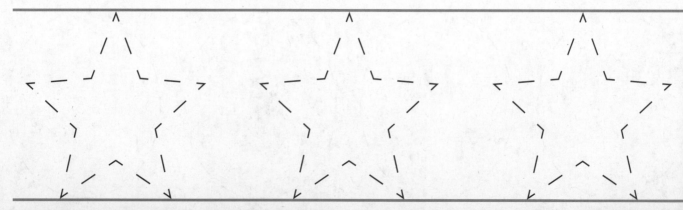

Tracing Shapes: Hearts

Trace the heart shapes. **Color** them to make more cookies.

Shapes on a Farm

Draw a line from each shape outline to the similar shapes in the farm picture.

Colorful Shapes

Color each shape inside the big box.
Use the list to help you choose the color for each shape.

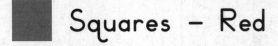 Squares – Red   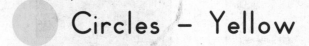 Circles – Yellow

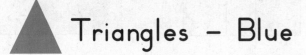 Triangles – Blue   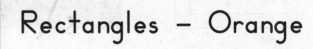 Rectangles – Orange

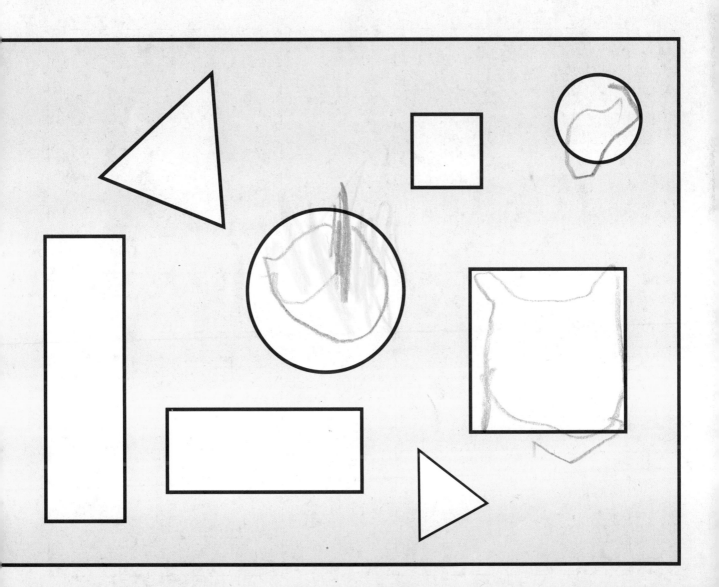

Squares Galore

Trace the squares. Then, **color** them to match the pictures.

Robot Shapes

How many of each shape can you find?
Count the shapes and **write** down the numbers in the boxes.

Which One Fits?

Draw a line from the shape inside the block to the matching shape outside.

Similar Shapes

Draw a line between objects with similar shapes.

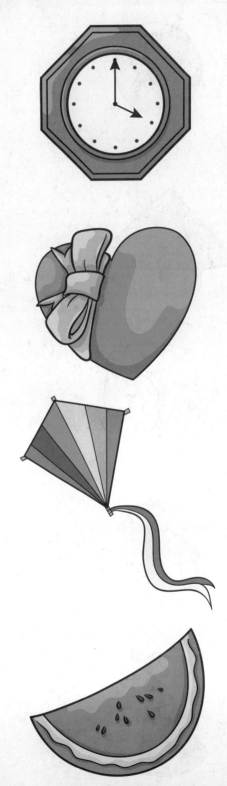

3D Shapes

Draw a line to connect each object and the shape it looks most like.

Blocks and Rectangles

Draw a line to connect each pair of blocks that will form a rectangle.

She Sells Seashells

Count the number of each type of shell. Write the number in the box.

Snowboard Fun

Use these directions to **color** the snowboards.

Tallest = [ ] blue   Shortest = [ ] yellow   Widest = [ ] purple   Skinniest = [ ] red

Pattern Perfect!

Draw the shape that would come next in the pattern.

_____

_____

_____

_____

_____

Find Those Shorts!

Cross out the swim trunks in each row that is different from the others.

Snow Symmetry

Draw a line to connect each snowflake to its missing half.

Butterfly Wings

Which of these butterflies is different from the others?
Find and **circle** it.

Little Leaves

Circle the two leaves in each row that match.

Rainy Day Match

Draw a line to connect the rain boots and their matching umbrellas.

Note Patterns

Finish the music patterns by **drawing** the note that comes next.

Colorful Caterpillar

Color the caterpillar by copying the color dot in each section.